COLLECTING SHAWNEE POTTERY
A Pictorial Reference And Price Guide

BY MARK E. SUPNICK

ISBN - 0-9611446-0-2

©
Copyright
1989

Eighth Printing 1995

Published By
L-W Book Sales
Box 69
Gas City, IN 46933

Printed by IMAGE GRAPHICS, INC., Paducah, Kentucky

Additional copies of this book may be ordered directly from the author.

MARK SUPNICK
2771 Oakbrook Manor
Ft. Lauderdale, FL 33332

$10.95 plus $2.00 for postage and handling

Additional writings by Mark E. Supnick

"COLLECTING HULL POTTERY'S LITTLE RED RIDING HOOD"

"WONDERFUL WORLD OF COOKIE JARS"

A pictorial reference and price guide

ISBN #0-9611446-1-0

2

ACKNOWLEDGEMENTS

Preparing an acknowledgement for a book is a trying experience at best. So many people have helped in so many ways.

First and foremost, I would like to thank my wife, Ellen, who throughout this writing has been a source of inspiration and encouragement to me.

My two sons deserve a special acknowledgement. Four year old Matthew runs ahead of me at every show advising the whole world that we're looking for "SHAWNEE." Todd, my ten year old son, is reponsible for a vast amount of my collection, since he has the ability to spot a piece of "SHAWNEE" at forty paces, in the darkest corner of any antique shop.

Probably the strongest motivating force in writing this book was Dan Huck. With Dan's enthusiasm, knowledge, and unselfishness, he has guided me through every segment of this book.

Dan has become a very special friend, with whom I will always debate which one of us has the largest collection.

I would like to express my deep gratitude to the many people who helped me in all phases of this book. Without their assistance, this book would not be possible.

Mark Supnick

INTRODUCTION

SHAWNEE POTTERY COMPANY has been formed for the creation, the manufacture and the distribution of Earthenware products.

On June 4th the Company acquired the Zanesville, Ohio, plant of the American Encaustic Tiling Company, Inc. Among the assets purchased were the various formulæ, research data and practical knowledge in Ceramic Art gained during many years of experience.

Since that time, new machinery and equipment have been purchased or constructed and are now being installed in the factory which is undergoing the alterations necessary to transform it into one of the most mechanically efficient and largest producers of Earthenware in the industry.

Ceramic engineers and designers have been engaged in research to produce the bodies, glazes, shapes and decorations that will be used. Unusual progress has been made in this work which is nearing completion. The body and glazes being developed will withstand extreme temperature changes. Resistance to heat and cold shock will extend beyond present standards for earthenware bodies and glazes. Glazes of varying texture will be produced in shades and tones of bright and pastel colors. Underglaze and overglaze decorations will be done by entirely new methods. The product will be light in weight and yet quite strong enough to meet all the requirements of hard usage in the home.

The policy of the company will be to develop a large volume of sales through broad consumer acceptance by creating and producing earthenware articles in a wide range of shapes and sizes, designed and styled in the modern mode, possessed of high quality and unusual durability, and sold at popular prices. The range of products to be manufactured will include useful Art Pottery; Bright Colored Dinnerware and Kitchenware; Lamp Bases; a large variety of specialties for ornamental purposes; specially designed products for packaging foods, chemicals and chemical combinations, and for premium requirements. A department will be maintained for the development of specialties to meet unusual needs.

The name and trademark of the Company were selected because the Shawnee tribe of American Indians once made the land adjoining the west bank of the Muskingum River their home and hunting ground. The site on which the factory is located is believed to have been a Shawnee village. These Indians were probably the first master craftsmen west of the Muskingum River in Ohio, and undoubtedly produced pottery from Zanesville clays long before white men settled the territory. The arrowhead in the trade mark is a duplicate of one found in the vicinity. It is an example of the craft of the Shawnee. The name is easily pronounced and associated with the trade mark will be remembered by the consumer from seeing their combination upon the product and in consumer advertising.

Operations will commence during August. About the same time, representatives of the company will begin calling on the trade and any courtesy extended them will be appreciated. Suggestions or advice relating to sizes and shapes of items, the decoration, treatment and styling, or any other matter of mutual interest will be gratefully received. The company hopes it will be favored with your patronage, and that a mutually satisfactory relationship will result.

You are extended a cordial invitation to visit the office and works at Zanesville after the 15th of September so you may see the facilities for manufacturing, the products, and the methods by which they are produced.

SHAWNEE POTTERY COMPANY

Reprinted from Shawnee's own Introduction Letter to the Trade. Issued September 1937.

INTRODUCTION *(Continued)*

Kitchen and Pantry Ware

Baked Apple Dishes	Coasters	Lipped Bowls	Salt Boxes
Baking Dishes	Coffee Pots and Drips	Marmalade Jars	Salad Forks
Beating Jars	Compartment Plates	Match Holders	Salad Spoons
Beverage Sets	Comports	Mugs	Salt and Pepper Shakers
Bottle Service Jars	Cookie Jars	Mustards	Saucers
Bowls (All sizes)	Cracker Jars	Nappies	Skillets
Butter Jars	Cups	Pie Plates	Steins
Cake Plates	Custard Cups	Pitchers	Tankards
Cake Servers	Egg Beaters	Pretzel Jars and Plates	Tea Pots
Carafes	Egg Cups	Pudding Dishes	Tom and Jerry Bowls and
Casseroles	Flour and Sugar Shakers	Ramekins	Mugs
Cereal and Spice Sets	Grease and Rouge Jars	Refrigerator Jars	Tumblers
Cheese Plates	Hors d'ouvre Plates	Relish Trays	Utility Trays
Chop Plates	Ice Tubs, Pots, Jars, Pitchers	Salad Bowls	Whipping Jars

As part of its sales policy, the company offers its customers a complete design and style service. Special articles will be made for special purposes and the designing department will be pleased to offer suggestions and advice relating to sizes and shapes of items, the decoration, treatment and style.

Decorative Art Pottery

Aquarium Ornaments	Coasters	Honey Jars	Rose Bowls
Animal Ornaments	Coffee Sets	Humidors	Salad Dishes
Ash Trays	Compartment Plates	Incense Burners	Service Plates
Berry Dishes	Cream Pitchers	Ivy Balls and Jars	Statues
Bilikins	Cups and Saucers	Jardiniers	Statuettes
Bird Bath Ornaments	Decanters	Lamp Bases	Strawberry Jars
Book Ends	Door Stops	Liqueur Sets	Sugar Jars
Boudoir Sets	Egg Dishes	Novelties	Tea Sets
Bridge Sets	Figurines	Nut Sets	Tobacco Jars and Covers
Bulb Bowls	Flower Blocks and Inserts	Oatmeals	Trays
Candelabra	Flower Pots and Saucers	Ornaments and What-Nots	Vases
Candle Holders	Fruit Bowls	Paper Weights	Wall Pockets
Cereal Dishes	Glazed Pots and Saucers	Plaques	
Clock Cases	Hanging Baskets	Platters	

Reprinted from Shawnee's own Introduction Letter to the Trade. Issued September 1937.

Dinner Ware

Bakers and Nappies (All sizes)
Bowls (All sizes)
Butters
Cake Plates
Casseroles

Coffees
Cups and Saucers
Covered Dishes
Creams
Cream Soups
Desserts

Dishes (All sizes)
Egg Cups
Fruits
Jugs and Covers
Oatmeals
Onion Soups

Pickles
Plates (All sizes)
Sugars
Teas
Tea Pots

SHAWNEE POTTERY COMPANY
ZANESVILLE, OHIO

●

Works and Offices

LOCATION: One mile North of U. S. Routes 22 and 40 on Linden Avenue, Zanesville, Ohio.

FLOOR SPACE IN BUILDINGS: 650,000 sq. ft., or 15 acres.

KILN CAPACITY: Three large Harrop Car Tunnel Kilns, Periodic and Decorating Kilns.

PRODUCTIVE CAPACITY: 100,000 articles each working day.

SHIPPING FACILITIES: Wheeling and Lake Erie, Pennsylvania, Baltimore & Ohio, and New York Central Railroads. Numerous motor transportation companies operating to all parts of the United States.

Reprinted from Shawnee's own Introduction Letter to the Trade. Issued September 1937.

6

Typical patent reports issued for products manufactured by the Shawnee Pottery Co.

140,203
DESIGN FOR A WATER JUG OR SIMILAR ARTICLE
Rudy V. Ganz, Zanesville, Ohio, assignor to Shawnee Pottery Co., Zanesville, Ohio
Application November 17, 1944, Serial No. 116,390
Term of patent 14 years
(Cl. D44—21)

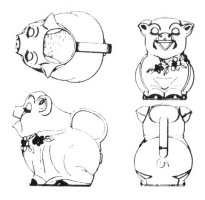

The ornamental design for a water jug or similar article, as shown.

139,092
DESIGN FOR A TEAPOT OR SIMILAR ARTICLE
Rudolph V. Ganz, Zanesville, Ohio, assignor to Shawnee Pottery Co., Zanesville, Ohio
Application June 29, 1944, Serial No. 114,256
Term of patent 14 years
(Cl. D44—26)

The ornamental design for a teapot or similar article, as shown.

141,323
DESIGN FOR A CONDIMENT SHAKER OR SIMILAR ARTICLE
Rudolph V. Ganz, Zanesville, Ohio, assignor to Shawnee Pottery Co., Zanesville, Ohio
Application February 28, 1945, Serial No. 118,187
Term of patent 14 years
(Cl. D44—22)

The ornamental design for a condiment shaker or similar article, as shown.

141,322
DESIGN FOR A COOKY JAR OR SIMILAR ARTICLE
Rudolph V. Ganz, Zanesville, Ohio, assignor to Shawnee Pottery Co., Zanesville, Ohio
Application February 28, 1945, Serial No. 118,186
Term of patent 14 years
(Cl. D58—25)

The ornamental design for a cooky jar or similar article, as shown.

Patent reports, courtesy of the "DEPRESSION GLASS DAZE" and Mrs. Lois Lehner.

(ADDITIONAL PATENTS NOT IN FIRST BOOK)

Typical Patent Reports Issued for Products Manufactured By The Shawnee Pottery Co.

149,625
DESIGN FOR A DARNER
Rolf J. Falk, Zanesville, Ohio, assignor to Shawnee Pottery Company, Zanesville, Ohio, a corporation of Ohio
Application June 5, 1947, Serial No. 139,456
Term of patent 14 years
(Cl. D3—19)

149,624
DESIGN FOR A LAMP BRACKET
Rolf J. Falk, Zanesville, Ohio, assignor to Shawnee Pottery Company, Zanesville, Ohio, a corporation of Ohio
Application March 7, 1947, Serial No. 137,440
Term of patent 14 years
(Cl. D48—4)

The ornamental design for a darner, as shown.

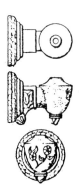

The ornamental design for a lamp bracket, as shown.

Patent Reports, Courtesy of Harvey Duke

(ADDITIONAL PATENTS NOT IN FIRST BOOK)

Typical Patent Reports Issued for Products Manufactured By The Shawnee Pottery Co.

12 - 2 - 47   148,012
DESIGN FOR A CHILD'S FEEDING SET
Rolf J. Falk, Zanesville, Ohio, assignor to Shaw-
nee Pottery Company, Zanesville, Ohio, a cor-
poration of Ohio
Application April 30, 1946, Serial No. 129,156
Term of patent 14 years
(Cl. D44—10)

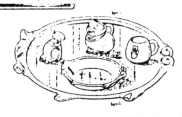

The ornamental design for a child's feeding set, as shown.

148,013
DESIGN FOR A CHILD'S FEEDING SET
Rolf J. Falk, Zanesville, Ohio, assignor to Shaw-
nee Pottery Company, Zanesville, Ohio, a cor-
poration of Ohio
Application April 30, 1946, Serial No. 129,157
Term of patent 14 years
(Cl. D44—10)

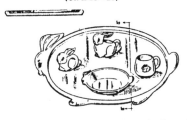

The ornamental design for a child's feeding set, as shown.

148,014
DESIGN FOR A CHILD'S FEEDING SET
Rolf J. Falk, Zanesville, Ohio, assignor to Shaw-
nee Pottery Company, Zanesville, Ohio, a cor-
poration of Ohio
Application April 30, 1946, Serial No. 129,158
Term of patent 14 years
(Cl. D44—10)

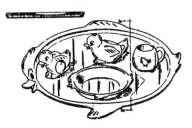

The ornamental design for a child's feeding set, as shown.

Patent Reports, Courtesy of Harvey Duke

These wonderful children's feeding sets seemed to be of limited production or were never put into production.

(ADDITIONAL PATENTS NOT IN FIRST BOOK)

Typical Patent Reports Issued for Products Manufactured
By The Shawnee Pottery Co.

141,324
**DESIGN FOR A TEAPOT OR SIMILAR
ARTICLE**
Rudolph V. Ganz, Zanesville, Ohio, assignor to
Shawnee Pottery Co., Zanesville, Ohio
Application February 28, 1945, Serial No. 118,188
Term of patent 14 years
(Cl. D44—26)

147,899
DESIGN FOR A CONDIMENT SHAKER
Rolf John Falk, Zanesville, Ohio, assignor to
Shawnee Pottery Company, Zanesville, Ohio, a
corporation of Ohio
Application April 20, 1946, Serial No. 128,806
Term of patent 14 years
(Cl. D44—22)

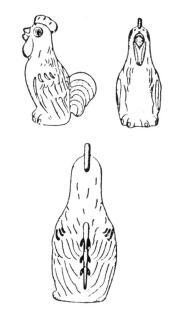

The ornamental design for a condiment shaker
or similar article, as shown.

The ornamental design for a teapot or similar
article, as shown.

Patent Reports, Courtesy of Harvey Duke

(ADDITIONAL PATENTS NOT IN FIRST BOOK)

Typical Patent Reports Issued for Products Manufactured By The Shawnee Pottery Co.

117,436
DESIGN FOR A TEAPOT
Rolf John Falk, Zanesville, Ohio, assignor to Shawnee Pottery Company, Zanesville, Ohio, a corporation of Ohio
Application April 20, 1946, Serial No. 128,808
Term of patent 14 years
(Cl. D44—26)

149,623
DESIGN FOR A TEAPOT
Rolf J. Falk, Zanesville, Ohio, assignor to Shawnee Pottery Company, Zanesville, Ohio, a corporation of Ohio
Application March 7, 1947, Serial No. 137,439
Term of patent 14 years
(Cl. D44—25)

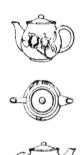

The ornamental design for a teapot, as shown.

The ornamental design for a teapot, as shown.

More Patents on pages 73, 74, 75

Patent Reports, Courtesy of Harvey Duke

PLATE 1

ROW 1
1. Man with pushcart marked USA 621.
2. Man with pushcart marked USA 621 advertising piece embossed "Rum Carioca."
3. Donkey with basket marked Shawnee 722.
4. Donkey with basket marked Shawnee 722.
5. Tulip vase marked USA 1115.

ROW 2
1. Mouse with cheese marked USA 705.
2. Mouse with cheese marked USA 705.
3. Boy with dog marked USA 582.
4. Boy with dog marked USA 582.
5. Boy with dog marked USA 582 with gold trim.
6. Shell planter marked USA 665.

ROW 3
1. Rickshaw planter marked USA 539.
2. Rickshaw planter marked USA 539 with gold trim.
3. Cherub planter marked USA 536.
4. Cherub planter marked USA 536 with gold trim.
5. Chick with cart marked Shawnee 720 with gold trim.
6. Tulip vase marked USA 1115 with gold trim.

ROW 4
1. Cockatiel planter marked Shawnee 523.
2. Cockatiel planter marked Shawnee 523 with gold trim and "Shafer" stamp.
3. Gazelle planter marked USA 613.

ROW 4 (continued)
4. Gazelle planter marked USA 613 with gold trim.
5. Fawn planter marked USA 535.
6. Fawn planter marked USA 535 with gold trim.

ROW 5
1. Donkey and cart marked USA 538 with gloss finish.
2. Donkey and cart marked USA 538 with matte finish and gold trim.
3. Clown planter marked USA 607.
4. Clown planter marked USA 607 with gold trim.
5. Frog on lily pad marked Shawnee 726.

ROW 6
1. Bud vase with embossed flowers marked USA 875.
2. Bud vase with embossed flowers marked USA 875.
3. Hound & Pekingese planter marked USA 611.
4. Hound & Pekingese planter marked USA 611 with gold trim.
5. Oriental with book marked USA 574.
6. Oriental with book marked USA 574 with gold trim.

ROW 7
1. Little elephant marked USA 759.
2. Little elephant marked USA 759.
3. Little elephant marked USA 759.
4. Pair of baby shoes planter marked USA.
5. Pair of baby shoes planter marked USA.
6. Bud vase marked USA.

PLATE 2

ROW 1
1. Oriental with umbrella bowl planter marked USA 701.
2. Oriental with umbrella bowl planter marked USA 701 with gold trim.
3. Flying goose planter marked Shawnee 820.
4. Elephant planter marked Shawnee USA.

ROW 2
1. Boy with wheelbarrow planter marked USA 750.
2. Boy with wheelbarrow planter marked USA 750.
3. Girl at well planter marked USA.
4. Bull planter marked Shawnee USA.

ROW 3
1. Dog planter marked USA.
2. Rockinghorse planter marked USA 526 with cold paint.
3. Rockinghorse planter marked USA 526.
4. Rockinghorse planter marked USA 526.

ROW 4
1. Bridge planter marked Shawnee 756.
2. Bridge planter marked Shawnee 756.
3. Hound planter marked USA.

ROW 5
1. Boy at fence no mark.
2. Boy at fence no mark with gold trim.
3. Boy at fence no mark with gold trim.
4. Girl at fence marked USA 581.
5. Boot marked USA.
6. Leather grain planter marked USA 885.
7. Leather grain planter marked USA 885.

ROW 6
1. Elf on shoe marked Shawnee 765.
2. Elf on shoe marked Shawnee 765 with gold trim.
3. Elf on shoe marked Shawnee 765.
4. Vase marked USA.
5. Vase marked USA.

ROW 7
1. Wheelbarrow with embossed flower marked USA.
2. Oriental with umbrella planter marked USA 617.
3. Oriental with umbrella planter marked USA 617 with gold trim.
4. Oriental with umbrella planter marked USA 617 with gold trim.
5. Leaf bud vase marked 1125.
6. Leaf bud vase marked 1125 with gold trim.

PLATE 3

ROW 1
1. Boy at stump marked USA 533.
2. Boy at stump marked USA 533 with gold trim.
3. Boy at stump marked USA 533.
4. Boy at stump marked USA 533 with gold trim.
5. Vase with wheat marked USA 1267.
6. Bud vase marked USA 1203.

ROW 2
1. Butterfly planter marked Shawnee USA 524.
2. Donkey pulling cart marked USA 709.
3. Donkey pulling cart marked USA 709.
4. Bud vase marked USA 1205.
5. Vase marked USA.

ROW 3
1. Pekingese at dog house marked Shawnee USA.
2. Pekingese at dog house marked Shawnee USA.
3. Chihuahua at dog house marked Shawnee USA.
4. Duck marked Shawnee USA 720.
5. Duck marked Shawnee USA 720 with gold trim and stamped "Shafer."

ROW 4
1. Tulip leaf planter marked Shawnee USA 466.
2. Bud vase marked Shawnee USA 865 with gold trim and decals.
3. Bud vase marked Shawnee USA 865 with gold trim and decals.
4. Push cart planter marked USA J544P.
5. Baby shoe planter marked USA.
6. Conch shell planter marked USA 241.

ROW 5
1. Pup on shoe planter marked USA (3 button variety).
2. Pup on shoe planter marked USA (3 button variety).
3. Pup on shoe planter marked USA (3 button variety).
4. Pup on shoe planter marked USA (3 button variety).
5. Girl watering flowers marked USA.

ROW 6
1. Pup on shoe marked USA (2 button variety).
2. Pup on shoe marked USA (2 button variety).
3. Pup on shoe marked USA (2 button variety).
4. Pup on shoe marked USA (2 button variety).
5. High heel shoe marked USA.

ROW 7
1. Cornucopia vase marked USA 835.
2. Cornucopia vase marked USA 835 with gold trim.
3. Cornucopia vase marked USA 835.
4. Cornucopia vase marked USA 835.
5. High heel shoe marked USA.

PLATE 4

ROW 1
1. Girl at basket marked USA 534.
2. Girl at basket marked USA 534 with gold trim.
3. Girl at basket marked USA 534.
4. Girl at basket marked USA 534 with gold trim.
5. Large watering can planter embossed with flowers marked USA.

ROW 2
1. Oriental figurine marked USA 602.
2. Oriental figurine marked USA 602 with gold trim.
3. Oriental figurine marked USA 602 with gold trim.
4. Oriental figurine with parasol marked USA 601.
5. Oriental figurine with parasol marked USA 601 with gold trim.
6. Oriental figurine with parasol marked USA 601 with gold trim.
7. Oriental boy with flowerpot marked USA 701.
8. Vase marked USA.

ROW 3
1. Donkey and cart marked USA.
2. Donkey and cart marked USA.
3. Donkey and cart marked USA.
4. Donkey and cart marked USA.
5. Donkey and cart marked USA.

ROW 4
1. Bird on planter marked Shawnee 767.
2. Bird on planter marked Shawnee 767.
3. Hound with jug marked Shawnee 610.

ROW 4 *(continued)*
4. Hound with jug marked Shawnee 610 with gold trim.
5. Swan bud vase marked USA 725.

ROW 5
1. Squirrel planter marked Shawnee 664.
2. Squirrel planter marked Shawnee 664 with gold trim.
3. Clown potholder marked USA 619.
4. Clown potholder marked USA 619 with gold trim.
5. Piano planter marked USA 528.
6. Bud vase marked USA 1125.

ROW 6
1. Donkey with basket planter marked USA 671.
2. Donkey with basket planter marked USA 671.
3. Dutch children at well planter marked Shawnee 710 with gold trim.
4. Vase with wheat marked USA with gold trim.

ROW 7
1. Dutch children at well planter marked Shawnee 710.
2. Dutch children at well planter marked Shawnee 710 with gold trim.
3. Dutch children at well planter marked Shawnee 710.

PLATE 5

ROW 1
1. Vase with iris marked USA.
2. Ram planter marked Shawnee 515.
3. Leaf vase marked USA 821.
4. Giraffe planter marked Shawnee 521.

ROW 2
1. Bowl planter marked USA.
2. Dog in boat planter marked Shawnee 736.
3. Bull planter marked Shawnee USA high gloss finish.
4. Pot planter with embossed flower marked USA.

ROW 3
1. Water troth planter marked USA 716 with gold trim.
2. Water troth planter marked USA 716.
3. Water troth planter marked USA 716.

ROW 4
1. Skunk planter marked Shawnee 512.
2. Skunk planter marked Shawnee 512.
3. Bowl planter marked Shawnee 160.
4. Bowl planter marked Shawnee 150.

ROW 5
1. Uncle Sam tophat planter marked USA.
2. Small bowl planter marked USA.
3. Small bowl planter marked USA.
4. Small bowl planter marked USA.
5. Ribbed vase with handles marked USA.
6. Ribbed vase with handles marked USA.

ROW 6
1. Open mouth fish planter marked USA.
2. Open mouth fish planter marked USA.
3. Open mouth fish planter marked USA.
4. Flowerpot with burlap texture no mark.
5. Flowerpot with liner burlap texture marked Shawnee.
6. Bud vase marked USA.

ROW 7
1. Duck pulling cart planter marked Shawnee 752.
2. Duck pulling cart planter marked Shawnee 752.
3. Duck pulling cart planter marked Shawnee 752.
4. Pair of candlestick holders marked USA.

PLATE 6

ROW 1
1. Horse planter marked Shawnee 506.
2. Embossed vase marked USA.
3. Four birds on a perch marked Shawnee 502.

ROW 2
1. Trellis planter or candy dish marked Shawnee 517.
2. Figural fawn planter marked Shawnee 737.
3. Figural fawn planter marked Shawnee 737.
4. Doe and fawn planter marked Shawnee 669.

ROW 3
1. Doe and fawn planter marked Shawnee 669.
2. Doe and fawn planter marked Shawnee 669.
3. Doe and fawn planter marked Shawnee 669 with gold trim.
4. Doe and fawn planter marked Shawnee 669 with gold trim.

ROW 4
1. Figural doe planter marked Shawnee 624.
2. Figural doe planter marked Shawnee 624.
3. Figural doe planter marked Shawnee 624.
4. Figural doe planter marked Shawnee 624.
5. Figural doe planter marked Shawnee 624 with gold trim.

ROW 5
1. Large vase embossed with flowers marked Shawnee 827.
2. Large vase embossed with flowers marked Shawnee 827.
3. Large vase embossed with flowers marked Shawnee 827.
4. Doe and log marked Shawnee 766.

PLATE 7

ROW 1
1. Globe planter marked Shawnee USA.
2. Globe planter marked Shawnee USA.
3. Boy at stump marked USA 532 (high stump variety).
4. Boy at stump marked USA 532 (low stump variety).
5. Dog planter marked USA.

ROW 2
1. Windmill planter marked Shawnee 715 with gold trim.
2. Windmill planter marked Shawnee 715 with gold trim.
3. Windmill planter marked Shawnee 715.
4. Bird planter marked USA.

ROW 3
1. Wheelbarrow planter with embossed flower marked USA.
2. Wheelbarrow planter marked USA.
3. Pig with wheelbarrow with embossed flower marked USA.
4. Basketweave planter marked Shawnee 444.
5. Cornucopia vase marked Shawnee 865.

ROW 4
1. Candlestick holder marked Shawnee 3026 trimmed in platinum.
2. Bowl planter marked 1704 with Shawnee paper label.
3. Girl at cornucopia bud vase marked USA 1275.
4. Boy at cornucopia bud vase marked USA 1265.
5. Embossed vase marked USA.

ROW 5
1. Flowerpot with liner marked Shawnee 484.
2. Flowerpot with liner marked Shawnee 484.
3. Flowerpot with liner marked Shawnee.
4. Bowl planter marked USA.
5. Bowl planter marked USA.
6. Planter marked Shawnee 455.

ROW 6
1. Children Who Lived In A Shoe planter marked USA 525.
2. Children Who Lived In A Shoe planter marked USA 525.
3. Children Who Lived In A Shoe planter marked USA 525.
4. Fan vase marked USA 1264.
5. Flowered vase marked USA 1225.

ROW 7
1. Flying goose planter marked USA 707.
2. Flying goose planter marked USA 707.
3. Cart planter marked USA 775.
4. Clock planter marked USA 1262.
5. Bull planter marked 668.

PLATE 8

ROW 1
1. Hand vase marked USA.
2. Hand vase marked USA.
3. Hand vase marked USA.
4. Hand vase marked USA.
5. Hand vase marked USA with gold trim.
6. High chair planter marked USA 727.
7. Flowerpot marked USA.

ROW 2
1. Lovebirds planter marked USA.
2. Lovebirds planter marked USA.
3. Rabbit with turnip planter marked USA 703.
4. Small goose planter marked USA.
5. Rabbit by stump planter marked USA 606.
6. Squirrel ashtray marked USA.

ROW 3
1. Ribbed planter with bird marked USA 502.
2. Smooth planter with bird no mark.
3. Watering can with embossed flower marked USA.
4. Coal bucket with embossed flower marked USA.
5. Coal bucket with embossed flower marked J541P.
6. Darning egg figurine no mark.

ROW 4
1. Embossed vase marked USA.
2. Shell planter marked Shawnee 154.
3. Shell planter marked Shawnee 154.
4. Pig planter marked USA 760.
5. Buddha planter marked USA 524.

ROW 5
1. Three pigs planter marked USA.
2. Small stagecoach planter marked USA 514.
3. Toy horse planter marked Shawnee 660.
4. Two Orientals carrying basket planter marked USA 537.
5. Embossed vase with handles marked USA.

ROW 6
1. Embossed bowl planter marked USA 182.
2. Embossed bowl planter marked USA 182 with gold trim.
3. Vase marked USA.
4. Vase marked USA.

ROW 7
1. Elephant planter marked USA.
2. Watering can planter marked USA.
3. Vase marked USA.
4. Two Orientals, one with mandolin marked USA 573.
5. Coal stove planter marked USA.

PLATE 9

ROW 1
1. Boy with chicken planter marked Shawnee 645.
2. Boy with chicken planter marked Shawnee 645.
3. Boy with chicken planter marked Shawnee 645 with gold trim.
4. Small pitcher marked USA 1168 with gold trim.
5. Small pitcher marked USA 1168.

ROW 2
1. Girl with basket of flowers planter marked USA 616.
2. Girl with basket of flowers planter marked USA 616.
3. Girl with basket of flowers planter marked USA 616 with gold trim.
4. Girl with basket of flowers planter marked USA 616 with gold trim.
5. Cat playing saxaphone planter marked Shawnee 729.
6. Bud vase marked USA 705.
7. Bud vase marked USA 705 in gold trim.

ROW 3
1. Locomotive planter marked USA 550.
2. Coal car planter marked USA.
3. Box car planter marked USA 552.
4. Caboose planter marked USA 553.
5. Caboose planter marked USA.
6. Rabbit at basket planter marked USA.

ROW 4
1. Open car planter marked USA 506 with gold trim (8 spoke variety).

ROW 4 (continued)
2. Open car planter marked USA 506 (8 spoke variety).
3. Open car planter marked USA 506 (8 spoke variety).
4. Crib planter marked USA J542P.
5. Crib planter marked USA 625.
6. Open mouth fish planter marked USA 845.

ROW 5
1. Open car planter marked USA 506 (4 spoke variety).
2. Open car planter marked USA 506 (4 spoke variety).
3. Open car planter marked USA 506 (4 spoke variety).
4. Poodle on bicycle planter marked USA 712.
5. House planter marked USA J543P.
6. Bud vase marked USA 1135.

ROW 6
1. Bird planter marked USA.
2. Bird planter marked USA.
3. Bird planter marked USA.
4. Basket planter marked USA 640.
5. Basket planter marked USA 640.

ROW 7
1. Bud vase marked USA 735.
2. Doe and fawn planter marked Shawnee 721.
3. Doe and fawn planter marked Shawnee 721.
4. Doe and fawn planter marked Shawnee 721 with gold trim.
5. Squirrel pulling acorn planter marked Shawnee 713.

PLATE 10

ROW 1
1-2. Pair of flying geese bookends marked Shawnee 4000.
3. Flying goose bookend marked Shawnee 4000 with gold trim.
4. Girl playing mandolin planter marked USA 576.

ROW 2
1. Circus animal cage planter marked USA.
2. Large leaf planter marked Shawnee 440.
3. Bowl planter marked USA 181.

ROW 3
1. Leaf bowl planter marked Shawnee 439.
2. Leaf bowl planter marked Shawnee 439.
3. Planter with liner marked USA.
4. Planter with liner marked USA.

ROW 4
1. Embossed planter with liner marked USA.
2. Gristmill planter marked Shawnee 769 with gold trim.
3. Gristmill planter marked Shawnee 769.
4. Gristmill planter marked Shawnee 769.

ROW 5
1. Dove planter marked Shawnee 2025.
2. Planter marked Shawnee 455.
3. Planter marked Shawnee 455.
4. Planter marked Shawnee 456.
5. Embossed planter marked USA.

ROW 6
1. Planter with liner marked Shawnee 534.
2. Planter with liner marked Shawnee 534.
3. Planter with liner marked Shawnee 534.
4. Planter with liner marked Shawnee 463.
5. Planter with liner marked Shawnee 463.

ROW 7
1. Planter with liner marked Shawnee 533.
2. Planter with liner marked Shawnee 533.
3. Planter with liner marked Shawnee 494.
4. Bow knot planter marked USA.
5. Planter with liner marked Shawnee 495.
6. Planter with liner marked Shawnee 495.

PLATE 11

ROW 1
1. Rooster planter marked Shawnee 503.
2. Rooster planter marked Shawnee 503.
3. Oriental at bamboo planter marked USA 702.
4. Oriental at bamboo planter marked USA 702 with gold trim.
5. Southern girl with umbrella planter marked USA 560.

ROW 2
1. Oriental with rickshaw marked USA.
2. Stage coach planter marked USA J545P.
3. Polynesian girl planter marked Shawnee 896.
4. Polynesian girl planter marked Shawnee 896.
5. Duck planter marked USA.

ROW 3
1. Two birds at nest planter marked USA.
2. Elf shoe planter marked Shawnee 765.
3. Elf shoe planter marked Shawnee 765 with gold trim.
4. Tractor trailer cab planter marked Shawnee 680.
5. Tractor trailer planter marked Shawnee 681.

ROW 4
1. Elf shoe planter marked Shawnee 765.
2. Elf shoe planter marked Shawnee 765 with gold trim.
3. Embossed planter with liner marked USA 455.

ROW 4 (continued)
4. Embossed planter with liner marked Shawnee.
5. Embossed planter with liner marked Shawnee.

ROW 5
1. Embossed planter with liner marked Shawnee 453.
2. Embossed planter with liner marked Shawnee.
3. Embossed planter with liner marked Shawnee.
4. Embossed planter with liner marked Shawnee.
5. Embossed planter with liner marked Shawnee 454.

ROW 6
1. Embossed planter with liner marked Shawnee 452.
2. Embossed planter with liner marked Shawnee 452.
3. Embossed planter with liner marked Shawnee 452.
4. Embossed planter with liner marked Shawnee 452.
5. Embossed planter with liner marked Shawnee 454.
6. Embossed planter with liner marked Shawnee 454.

ROW 7
1. Bow knot planter marked USA.
2. Bow knot planter marked USA.
3. Bow knot planter marked USA.
4. Embossed planter with liner marked Shawnee 465.
5. Embossed planter with liner marked USA.
6. Small bowl planter marked USA.

PLATE 12

ROW 1
1. Birds at bird house wall pocket marked USA 830.
2. Birds at bird house wall pocket marked USA 830.
3. Birds at bird house wall pocket marked USA 830 with gold trim.
4. Birds at bird house wall pocket marked USA 830 with gold trim.
5. Bow knot wall pocket marked USA 434.

ROW 2
1. Girl with rag doll wall pocket marked USA 810.
2. Girl with rag doll wall pocket marked USA 810.
3. Girl with rag doll wall pocket marked USA 810 with gold trim.
4. Grandfather clock wall pocket marked USA 1261.
5. Grandfather clock wall pocket marked USA 1261 with gold trim.

ROW 3
1. Telephone wall pocket marked USA 529.
2. Clock wall pocket marked USA 530.
3. Clock wall pocket marked USA 530 with gold trim.
4. Little Jack Horner wall pocket marked USA 585.
5. Little Bo Peep wall pocket marked USA 586.

ROW 4
1. Stage coach planter marked Shawnee 733.
2. Bow knot planter marked Shawnee 518 with gold trim.
3. Bowl planter marked Shawnee 163.

ROW 5
1. Stage coach planter marked Shawnee 733.
2. Stage coach planter marked Shawnee 733 with gold trim.
3. Bowl planter marked USA 1703 with paper Shawnee label.

PLATE 13

ROW 1
1. Swan vase marked USA 806.
2. Swan vase marked USA 806.
3. Swan vase marked USA 806 with gold trim.
4. Swan vase marked USA 806.
5. Swan vase marked USA 806.

ROW 2
1. Vase embossed with philodendron leaves marked Shawnee 805.
2. Vase embossed with philodendron leaves marked Shawnee 805 with gold trim.
3. Vase embossed with philodendron leaves marked Shawnee 805.
4. Large hand vase marked USA.
5. Large hand vase marked USA.
6. Vase marked USA.

ROW 3
1. Ribbed vase marked USA 809 with gold trim.
2. Ribbed vase marked USA 809.
3. Ribbed vase marked USA 809.
4. Bud vase with handle marked USA 1178.
5. Bud vase with handle marked USA 1178 with gold trim.
6. Bud vase with handle marked USA 1178.
7. Bud vase with handle marked USA 1178.

ROW 4
1. Bow knot vase marked USA 819.
2. Bow knot vase marked USA 819.
3. Bow knot vase marked USA 819.
4. Bow knot vase marked USA 819.
5. Bow knot vase marked USA 819.

PLATE 14

ROW 1
1. Dolphin vase marked Shawnee 828.
2. Dolphin vase marked Shawnee 828.
3. Large vase marked Shawnee USA.
4. Vase marked USA.
5. Vase marked USA.

ROW 2
1. Ribbed vase marked USA.
2. Ribbed vase marked USA.
3. Large scalloped planter marked Shawnee 436.
4. Large scalloped planter marked Shawnee 436.
5. Tall vase marked USA.

ROW 3
1. Leaf vase marked Shawnee 823.
2. Leaf vase marked Shawnee 823.
3. Leaf vase marked Shawnee 823 with gold trim and "Shafer" stamp.
4. Canopy bed planter marked Shawnee 734.

ROW 4
1. Gazelle with baby planter marked Shawnee 841.
2. Large vase marked Shawnee 890.
3. Large vase marked Shawnee 890.
4. Duck planter marked USA.

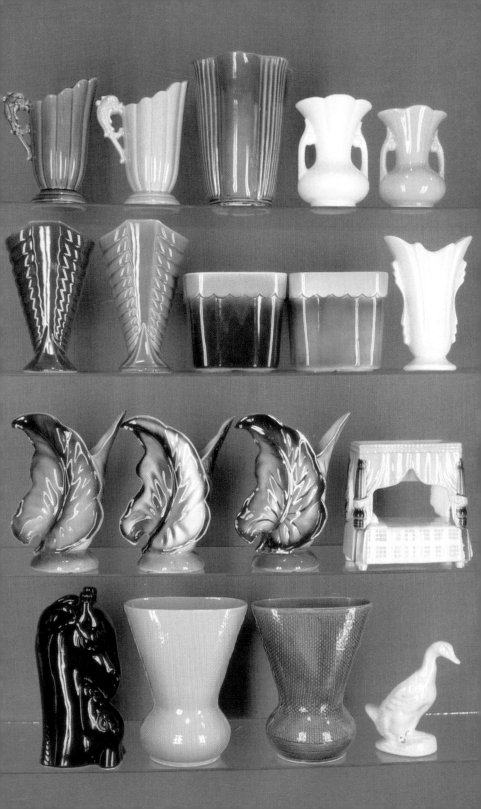

PLATE 15

ROW 1
1. Cornucopia vase marked USA.
2. Cornucopia vase marked USA.
3. Cornucopia vase marked USA.
4. Cornucopia vase marked USA.

ROW 2
1. Scalloped vase marked Shawnee.
2. Scalloped vase marked Shawnee.
3. Scalloped vase marked Shawnee.
4. Scalloped vase marked Shawnee with gold trim.
5. Frog playing guitar planter marked USA.
6. Frog playing guitar planter marked USA.

ROW 3
1. Pitcher marked USA 808.
2. Pitcher marked USA 808.
3. Pineapple vase marked Shawnee 839.
4. Pineapple vase marked Shawnee 839 with gold trim.
5. Pineapple vase marked Shawnee 839.
6. Vase marked USA.

ROW 4
1. Doe in shadowbox vase marked Shawnee 850.
2. Doe in shadowbox vase marked Shawnee 850.
3. Doe in shadowbox vase marked Shawnee 850.
4. Doe in shadowbox vase marked Shawnee 850.
5. Doe in shadowbox vase marked Shawnee 850.

PLATE 16

ROW 1
1. Fish planter marked USA 717.
2. Fish planter marked USA 717 with gold trim.
3. Large embossed vase marked USA.

ROW 2
1. Fish planter marked USA 717.
2. Gazelle figurine (not a planter) marked USA 614.
3. Embossed vase marked USA.

ROW 3
1. Dove vase marked USA 829.
2. Dove vase marked USA 829 with gold trim.
3. Dove vase marked USA 829.
4. Large burlap textured vase marked Shawnee 880.

ROW 4
1. Gazelle planter marked Shawnee 840 (matte finish).
2. Gazelle planter marked Shawnee 840 (gloss finish).
3. Large leaf planter marked USA 822.
4. Large leaf planter marked USA 822 with gold trim and "Shafer" stamp.

PLATE 17

ROW 1
1. Smiley pig pitcher marked pat. Smiley.
2. Smiley pig pitcher marked pat. Smiley.
3. Smiley pig pitcher marked pat. Smiley.
4. Smiley pig pitcher marked pat. Smiley, stamped "LeMieux China" hand decorated and gilt entirely in platinum.

ROW 2
1. Smiley pig pitcher marked pat. Smiley with gold trim and hand decoration.
2. Smiley pig pitcher marked pat. Smiley with gold trim and hand decoration.
3. Smiley pig pitcher marked pat. Smiley with gold trim and hand decoration.
4. Charlicleer pitcher marked pat. Charlicleer.

ROW 3
1. Charlicleer pitcher marked pat. Charlicleer with gold trim, decals and hand decorations.
2. Charlicleer pitcher marked pat. Charlicleer with gold trim and hand decoration.
3. Charlicleer pitcher marked pat. Charlicleer with gold trim, decals and hand decorations.
4. Charlicleer pitcher marked pat. Charlicleer gilt entirely in gold.

ROW 4
1. Little Boy Blue pitcher marked Shawnee 46 with gold trim.
2. Little Bo Peep pitcher marked Shawnee 47 with gold trim.
3. Goblet trimmed entirely in gold to match gilt Charlicleer pitcher marked hand decorated 24K gold.
4. Goblet trimmed entirely in platinum to match gilt Smiley Pig pitcher marked "LeMieux China" hand decorated in platinum.
5. Little Boy Blue pitcher marked Shawnee 46.
6. Little Bo Peep pitcher marked Shawnee 47.

PLATE 18

ROW 1
1. Cookie house sugar bowl marked USA 8.
2. Cookie house teapot marked USA 7.
3. Cookie house salt and peppers marked USA 9.
4. Decorative kitchen set marked as follows: Large salt and peppers marked USA, sugar bowl marked USA, small salt and peppers no mark.
5. Cookie house cookie jar (not illustrated) to match items No. 1, 2, 3, marked USA 6.

ROW 2
1. Fruit cookie jar or casserole marked Shawnee 84.
2. Fruit casserole marked Shawnee 83.
3. Fruit casserole marked Shawnee 81.
4. Fruit pitcher marked Shawnee 80.
5. Fruit salt and pepper set marked Shawnee 82.

ROW 3
1. Jug salt and peppers marked with Shawnee paper label.
2. Matching pitcher marked USA.
3. Matching teapot marked USA.
4. Teapot marked USA.

ROW 4
1. Large daisy salt and peppers marked USA.
2. Daisy pitcher marked USA.
3. Daisy creamer marked USA.
4. Small daisy salt shaker no mark.
5. Drummer boy cookie jar marked USA 10.

PLATE 19

ROW 1
1. Winnie The Pig cookie jar marked pat. Winnie USA.
2. Winnie The Pig cookie jar marked USA.
3. Winnie The Pig cookie jar marked pat. Winnie USA.
4. Winnie The Pig cookie jar marked USA.

ROW 2
1. Winnie The Pig cookie jar marked pat. Winnie USA with gold trim and hand decoration.
2. Winnie The Pig cookie jar marked pat. Winnie USA with gold trim and hand decoration.
3. Lucky elephant cookie jar marked USA with gold trim and decals.
4. Lucky elephant cookie jar marked USA.

ROW 3
1. Mugsey cookie jar marked pat. Mugsey USA with gold trim and decals.
2. Mugsey cookie jar marked pat. Mugsey USA with gold trim.
3. Mugsey cookie jar marked USA.
4. Winnie The Pig cookie jar bank marked Shawnee Winnie 61 with gold trim.

ROW 4
1. Smiley pig cookie jar bank marked Shawnee Smiley 60.
2. Winnie The Pig cookie jar bank marked Shawnee Winnie 61.
3. Smiley pig cookie jar bank marked Shawnee Smiley 60.
4. Winnie The Pig cookie jar bank marked Shawnee Winnie 61.

PLATE 20

ROW 1
1. Smiley pig cookie jar marked USA.
2. Smiley pig cookie jar marked USA.
3. Smiley pig cookie jar marked USA.
4. Smiley pig cookie jar marked USA.

ROW 2
1. Smiley pig cookie jar marked USA with gold trim and flower decals.
2. Smiley pig cookie jar marked USA with gold trim and flower decals with additional flowers on bib.
3. Smiley pig cookie jar marked USA with gold trim.
4. Smiley pig cookie jar marked USA with gold trim and flower decals.

ROW 3
1. Smiley pig cookie jar marked USA with gold trim.
2. Smiley pig cookie jar marked USA with gold trim and flower decals.
3. Smiley pig cookie jar marked USA with gold trim.
4. Smiley pig cookie jar marked USA with gold trim and flower decals.

ROW 4
1. Smiley pig cookie jar marked pat. Smiley Pig.
2. Smiley pig cookie jar marked USA.
3. Clown cookie jar marked Shawnee 12 with gold trim.
4. Clown cookie jar marked Shawnee 12.

PLATE 21

ROW 1
1. Dutch girl cookie jar marked USA.
2. Dutch girl cookie jar marked USA with gold trim, gold decals, and paper label.
3. Dutch girl cookie jar marked USA with gold trim and flower decal.
4. Dutch girl cookie jar marked USA.

ROW 2
1. Dutch girl cookie jar marked USA.
2. Dutch girl cookie jar marked USA.
3. Dutch girl cookie jar marked USA.
4. Jug cookie jar marked USA 75.

ROW 3
1. Dutch girl cookie jar marked Great Northern 1026.
2. Dutch boy cookie jar marked Great Northern 1025.
3. Dutch girl cookie jar marked Great Northern 1026.
4. Little Chef cookie jar marked USA.

ROW 4
1. Puss-N-Boots cookie jar marked pat. Puss-N-Boots.
2. Puss-N-Boots cookie jar marked pat. Puss-N-Boots with gold trim and flower decals.
3. Puss-N-Boots cookie jar marked pat. Puss-N-Boots with gold trim and flower decals.
4. Puss-N-Boots cookie jar marked pat. Puss-N-Boots with gold trim and flower decals (variety 2 note position of tail over boot).

PLATE 22

ROW 1
1. Owl cookie jar marked USA with gold trim.
2. Owl cookie jar marked USA.
3. Dutch boy cookie jar marked USA with gold trim and patches with paper label.
4. Dutch boy cookie jar marked USA.

ROW 2
1. Dutch boy cookie jar marked USA with gold trim and flower decals.
2. Dutch boy cookie jar marked USA with gold trim and patches.
3. Dutch boy cookie jar marked USA.
4. Dutch boy cookie jar marked USA.

ROW 3
1. Dutch boy cookie jar marked USA with gold trim and flower decals.
2. Dutch boy cookie jar marked USA with gold trim and flower decals.
3. Dutch boy cookie jar marked USA.
4. Sailor boy cookie jar marked USA with gold trim and flower decals, with paper label.

ROW 4
1. Elephant ice server marked Shawnee 60.
2. Elephant ice server marked Shawnee 60.
3. Octagon cookie jar marked USA.
4. Sailor boy cookie jar marked USA.

PLATE 23

ROW 1
1. Pair of farmer pig salt and peppers.
2. Pair of farmer pig salt and peppers with gold trim.
3. Pair of Puss-N-Boots salt and peppers with gold trim.
4. Pair of Puss-N-Boots salt and peppers with gold trim.
5. Pair of Puss-N-Boots salt and peppers.

ROW 2
1. Pair of duck salt and peppers marked with paper label.
2. Pair of milk can salt and peppers marked with paper label.
3. Pair of Sailor Boy and Bo Peep salt and peppers.
4. Pair of Sailor Boy and Bo Peep salt and peppers with gold trim.
5. Pair of small Mugsey salt and peppers.
6. Smiley Pig salt shaker with gold trim.

ROW 3
1. Pair of wheelbarrow salt and peppers.
2. Pair of owl salt and peppers.
3. Pair of owl salt and peppers with green eyes and marked USA.
4. Pair of owl salt and peppers with gold trim.
5. Pair of Winnie salt and peppers.

ROW 4
1. Pair of Winnie salt and peppers.
2. Pair of Winnie salt and peppers.
3. Pair of Winnie salt and peppers.
4. Pair of Smiley salt and peppers.
5. Pair of Smiley salt and peppers.

ROW 5
1. Pair of Smiley salt and peppers.
2. Matching pair of Winnie and Smiley salt and peppers.
3. Pair of Winnie salt and peppers with gold trim.
4. Matching pair of Winnie and Smiley salt and peppers with gold trim.
5. Smiley salt shaker with gold trim.

ROW 6
1. Pair of watering can salt and peppers.
2. Pair of watering can salt and peppers with gold trim.
3. Pair of small Charlicleer salt and peppers.
4. Pair of small Mugsey salt and peppers with gold trim.

ROW 7
1. Winnie salt shaker with gold trim.
2. Smiley salt shaker.
3. Smiley salt shaker.
4. Pair of white corn sugar shakers marked USA.
5. Pair of 5¼" corn salt and peppers.
6. Pair of 3¼" corn salt and peppers.

PLATE 24

ROW 1
1. Pair of Dutch children salt and peppers with gold trim.
2. Pair of Dutch children salt and peppers.
3. Pair of Swiss children salt and peppers.
4. Pair of Swiss children salt and peppers with gold trim.

ROW 2
1. Pair of Dutch boy and Dutch girl salt and peppers with gold trim and flower decals.
2. Pair of large Charlicleer salt and peppers.
3. Pair of large Mugsey salt and peppers with gold trim.
4. Pair of large Mugsey salt and peppers.

ROW 3
1. Pair of flowerpot salt and peppers.
2. Pair of flowerpot salt and peppers with gold trim.
3. Pair of flowerpot salt and peppers with gold trim.
4. Pair of milk can salt and peppers with gold trim and flower decals.
5. Dutch girl salt shaker.

ROW 4
1. Pair of Smiley Pig salt and peppers with gold trim.
2. Pair of S & P salt and peppers with gold trim.
3. Pair of S & P salt and peppers with gold trim.
4. Pair of S & P salt and peppers.
5. Pair of small fruit salt and peppers marked USA 82 with gold trim.

ROW 5
1. Pair of Smiley Pig salt and peppers.
2. Pair of Smiley Pig salt and peppers.
3. Pair of Smiley Pig salt and peppers.
4. Pair of Smiley Pig salt and peppers.

ROW 6
1. Pair of Smiley Pig salt and peppers.
2. Pair of Smiley Pig salt and peppers with gold trim and flower decals.
3. Pair of Smiley Pig salt and peppers with gold trim and flower decals.
4. Pair of Winnie The Pig salt and peppers.

ROW 7
1. Pair of Winnie The Pig salt and peppers.
2. Dutch girl salt shaker.
3. Pair of Dutch boy and Dutch girl salt and peppers.
4. Pair of large fruit salt and peppers marked USA 8.
5. Smiley Pig salt shaker with gold trim.

PLATE 25

ROW 1
1. Granny Anne teapot marked USA.
2. Granny Anne teapot marked pat. Granny Anne.
3. Granny Anne teapot marked USA.
4. Granny Anne teapot marked USA with gold trim and flower decals.

ROW 2
1. Granny Anne teapot marked pat. Granny Anne with gold trim and gold decals.
2. Granny Anne teapot marked pat. Granny Anne with gold trim and flower decals.
3. Bo Peep pitcher marked pat. Bo Peep.
4. Bo Peep pitcher marked pat. Bo Peep.

ROW 3
1. Bo Peep pitcher marked pat. Bo Peep with gold trim and flower decals.
2. Bo Peep pitcher marked pat. Bo Peep with gold trim.
3. Bo Peep pitcher marked pat. Bo Peep with gold trim and flower decals.
4. Bo Peep pitcher marked pat. Bo Peep with gold trim and flower decals.

ROW 4
1. Tom Tom teapot marked Tom The Piper's Son 44.
2. Tom Tom teapot marked Tom The Piper's Son with gold trim and patches on his pants.
3. Tom Tom teapot marked Tom The Piper's Son 44 with gold trim.
4. Tom Tom teapot marked Tom The Piper's Son.

PLATE 26

ROW 1
1. Clover flower teapot marked USA.
2. Clover flower sugar bowl marked USA.
3. Water bucket sugar bowl to match Dutch boy and Dutch girl marked USA.
4. Elephant teapot marked USA.
5. Elephant teapot marked USA. Lid not shown.

ROW 2
1. Coffee pot marked USA.
2. Teapot marked USA with gold trim.
3. Teapot marked USA.
4. Lobster creamer marked Shawnee 909 with paper label.

ROW 3
1. Teapot marked USA.
2. Teapot marked USA with gold trim.
3. Teapot marked USA.
4. Teapot marked USA.

ROW 4
1. Pitcher marked USA 32.
2. Pitcher marked USA 40.
3. Pitcher marked USA 40 with gold trim.
4. Pitcher marked USA 35.

PLATE 27

ROW 1
1. Teapot marked USA.
2. Sugar bowl marked USA.
3. Creamer marked USA.
4,6. Pair of salt and peppers.
5. Pitcher marked USA.

These items, shown on opposite page, are corn pattern with a white and green glaze. Reportedly they were given as a premium from one of the large soap companies.

ROW 2
1. Smiley creamer marked pat. Smiley.
2. Smiley creamer marked pat. Smiley with gold trim.
3. Smiley creamer marked Shawnee 86.
4. Smiley creamer marked Shawnee 86 with gold trim.
5. Smiley creamer marked pat. Smiley.

ROW 3
1. Puss-N-Boots creamer marked Shawnee 85.
2. Puss-N-Boots creamer marked Shawnee 85 with gold trim.
3. Puss-N-Boots creamer marked pat. Puss-N-Boots.
4. Puss-N-Boots creamer marked pat. Puss-N-Boots.
5. Puss-N-Boots creamer marked pat. Puss-N-Boots with gold trim.

ROW 4
1. Puss-N-Boots creamer marked pat. Puss-N-Boots with gold trim and flower decals.
2. Puss-N-Boots creamer marked pat. Puss-N-Boots gilt entirely in gold.

ROW 4 (continued)
3. Elephant creamer marked pat. USA with gold trim and flower decals.
4. Elephant creamer marked pat. USA.

ROW 5
1. Set of four coaster ashtrays marked USA 411 with paper label.
2. Bull dog bank marked with paper label.
3. Tumbling bear bank marked with paper label.

ROW 6
1. Tumbling bear figurine.
2. Teddy bear figurine.
3. Pekingese figurine.
4. Puppy figurine.
5. Rabbit figurine marked with paper label.

PLATE 28

ROW 1
1. Pair of 5¼" salt and peppers.
2. Pair of 3¼" salt and peppers.
3. Relish tray marked Shawnee 79.
4. Individual casserole marked Shawnee 73.
5. Covered butter dish marked Shawnee 72.
6. Utility jar or sugar bowl marked Shawnee 78.
7. Creamer marked Shawnee 70.

ROW 2
1. 5" mixing bowl marked Shawnee 5.
2. 6¼" mixing bowl marked Shawnee 6.
3. 8" mixing bowl marked Shawnee 8.
4. 12" platter marked Shawnee 96.
5. 9" vegetable dish marked Shawnee 95.
6. 10 oz. teapot marked Shawnee 65.

ROW 3
1. Soup-cereal bowl marked Shawnee 94.
2. 6" fruit dish marked Shawnee 92.
3. 8" salad plate marked Shawnee 93.
4. Cup and saucer marked as follows: cup 90, saucer 91.
5. 10" plate marked Shawnee 68.
6. Three piece range set catalog No. 7778.

ROW 4
1. Cookie jar marked Shawnee 66.
2. Hot coffee jug marked Shawnee 71.
3. Large casserole marked Shawnee 74.
4. 8 oz. mug marked Shawnee 69.
5. 30 oz. teapot marked Shawnee 75.

Plate 28 is a reproduction from a catalog issued by Shawnee to the trade approximately 1957. This catalog compliments of Mr. John Bonistal, past president of the Shawnee Co.

77 — 5½" Salt and
Pepper Shakers
1 doz. pairs. Wt. 16 lbs.

76 — 3½" Salt and
Pepper Shakers
2 doz. pairs. Wt. 12 lbs.

73 — 9 oz.
Individual Casserole
1 doz. to carton
Wt. 16½ lbs.

79 — Relish Tray or
Spoon Holder
2 doz. to carton
Wt. 16½ lbs.

72 — Covered Butter Dish
1 doz. to carton
Wt. 19 lbs.

78 — 14 oz. Utility Jar
1 doz. per carton
Wt. 18 lbs.

70 — 12 oz. Jug
2 doz. per carton
Wt. 17 lbs.

70/78 — Sugar and Creamer set
12 sets per carton. Wt. 26 lbs.

5 — 5" Mixing Bowl
4 doz. per carton
Wt. 38 lbs.

6 — 6½" Mixing Bowl
3 doz. per carton
Wt. 44 lbs.

8 — 8" Mixing Bowl
2 doz. per carton
Wt. 60 lbs.

96 — 12" Platter
1 doz. to carton
Wt. 25 lbs.

95 — 9" Vegetable Dish
1 doz. to carton
Wt. 23 lbs.

65 — 10 oz. Tea Pot
1 doz. to carton
Wt. 10½ lbs.

94 — Soup-Cereal Bowl
2 doz. to carton
Wt. 28 lbs.

92 — 6" Fruit Dish
2 doz. to carton
Wt. 16 lbs.

93 — 8" Salad-Dessert Plate
2 doz. to carton. Wt. 20 lbs.

90 — 5 oz. Cup
2 doz. to carton
Wt. 12 lbs.

91 — 5½" Saucer
2 doz. to carton
Wt. 8 lbs.

90/91 — Cup and Saucer
2 doz. to carton. Wt. 20 lbs.

68 — 10" Plate
1 doz. to carton
Wt. 20½ lbs.

7778 — 3 piece Range Set
pretties any stove
12 sets per carton
Wt. 34 lbs.

66 — Cookie Jar holds 2 lb. cookies
½ doz. to carton. Wt. 35 lbs.

71 — Jug holds quart of hot coffee
1 doz. per carton. Wt. 28 lbs.

74 — 1½ Quart
covered Casserole ovenproof
1 doz. per carton. Wt. 49 lbs.

69 — 8 oz. Mug
2 doz. to carton
Wt. 14½ lbs.

75 — 30 oz. Tea Pot
1 doz. per carton
Wt. 30 lbs.

1993 PRICE GUIDE

PLATE 1

Row 1.	1. $30-40	2. $40-50	3. $25-50	4. $25-50	5. $15-20
Row 2.	1. $30-35	2. $30-35	3. $10-15	4. $8-10	5. $20-25 6. $15-20
Row 3.	1. $15-20	2. $20-25	3. $10-15	4. $20-22	5. $40-50 6. $15-20
Row 4.	1. $15-20	2. $20-25	3. $25-30	4. $35-40	5. $10-15 6. $20-25
Row 5.	1. $15-20	2. $20-25	3. $25-30	4. $30-35	5. $35-40
Row 6.	1. $15-20	2. $15-20	3. $15-20	4. $10-15	5. $15-20 6. $25-30
Row 7.	1. $20-25	2. $20-25	3. $20-25	4. $5-10	5. $5-10 6. $5-10

PLATE 2

Row 1.	1. $15-20	2. $20-25	3. $25-30	4. $50-75	
Row 2.	1. $20-25	2. $20-25	3. $10-15	4. $50-75	
Row 3.	1. $10-15	2. $25-35	3. $25-35	4. $25-35	
Row 4.	1. $20-25	2. $20-25	3. $15-20		
Row 5.	1. $10-15	2. $20-25	3. $20-25	4. $15-20	5. $10-12 6. $15-18
	7. $15-18				
Row 6.	1. $20-25	2. $35-45	3. $20-25	4. $5-10	5. $5-10
Row 7.	1. $15-20	2. $20-25	3. $20-25	4. $10-15	5. $15-20 6. $25-30

PLATE 3

Row 1.	1. $10-15	2. $20-25	3. $10-15	4. $20-25	5. $20-25 6. $15-18
Row 2.	1. $10-15	2. $30-35	3. $30-35	4. $25-30	5. $8-10
Row 3.	1. $30-35	2. $20-25	3. $20-25	4. $35-45	5. $35-50
Row 4.	1. $15-20	2. $30-35	3. $30-35	4. $25-30	5. $8-10 6. $15-20
Row 5.	1. $15-20	2. $15-20	3. $15-20	4. $15-20	5. $15-20
Row 6.	1. $15-20	2. $15-20	3. $15-20	4. $15-20	5. $15-20
Row 7.	1. $15-20	2. $20-25	3. $15-20	4. $15-20	5. $15-20

PLATE 4

Row 1.	1. $15-20	2. $25-30	3. $15-20	4. $20-25	5. $15-20
Row 2.	1. $18-20	2. $20-25	3. $18-20	4. $15-20	5. $15-20 6. $15-20
	7. $15-20	8. $8-10			
Row 3.	1. $15-20	2. $15-20	3. $15-20	4. $15-20	5. $15-20
Row 4.	1. $20-25	2. $20-25	3. $15-20	4. $25-30	5. $15-20
Row 5.	1. $10-15	2. $20-25	3. $30-35	4. $35-40	5. $35-40 6. $8-10
Row 6.	1. $25-30	2. $25-30	3. $25-30	4. $20-30	
Row 7.	1. $20-25	2. $25-30	3. $20-25		

PLATE 5

Row 1.	1. $10-15	2. $20-25	3. $15-20	4. $30-35	
Row 2.	1. $10-12	2. $25-30	3. $50-75	4. $8-10	
Row 3.	1. $30-35	2. $25-30	3. $25-30		
Row 4.	1. $30-35	2. $30-35	3. $8-10	4. $8-10	
Row 5.	1. $10-12	2. $5-10	3. $5-10	4. $5-10	5. $10-12 6. $10-12
Row 6.	1. $10-15	2. $10-15	3. $10-15	4. $5-10	5. $5-10 6. $6-8
Row 7.	1. $25-30	2. $25-30	3. $25-30	4. $25-30 per pair	

PLATE 6

Row 1.	1. $50-70	2. $10-15	3. $50-70		
Row 2.	1. $20-25	2. $30-35	3. $30-35	4. $30-35	
Row 3.	1. $30-35	2. $30-35	3. $35-40	4. $35-40	
Row 4.	1. $30-35	2. $30-35	3. $30-35	4. $30-35	5. $35-40
Row 5.	1. $35-40	2. $35-40	3. $35-40	4. $50-60	

PLATE 7

Row 1.	1. $25-35	2. $25-35	3. $15-20	4. $20-25	5. $20-25
Row 2.	1. $35-45	2. $35-45	3. $25-30	4. $12-15	
Row 3.	1. $5-10	2. $5-10	3. $5-10	4. $5-10	5. $5-10
Row 4.	1. $35-40	2. $15-20	3. $15-20	4. $15-20	5. $5-10
Row 5.	1. $5-10	2. $5-10	3. $5-10	4. $5-10	5. $5-10 6. $5-10
Row 6.	1. $20-25	2. $20-25	3. $20-25	4. $20-25	5. $20-25
Row 7.	1. $25-35	2. $25-35	3. $15-20	4. $25-35	5. $20-30

PLATE 8

Row 1.	1. $15-20	2. $15-20	3. $15-20	4. $15-20	5. $40-50 6. $60-100
	7. $10-12				
Row 2.	1. $15-20	2. $15-20	3. $30-35	4. $15-20	5. $15-20 6. $30-35
Row 3.	1. $15-20	2. $15-20	3. $18-20	4. $18-20	5. $15-20 6. $50-60
Row 4.	1. $8-10	2. $10-15	3. $10-15	4. $25-30	5. $25-30
Row 5.	1. $15-20	2. $15-20	3. $20-25	4. $10-15	5. $8-10
Row 6.	1. $15-20	2. $20-25	3. $5-10	4. $5-10	
Row 7.	1. $25-30	2. $15-20	3. $5-10	4. $10-15	5. 20-25

PLATE 9

Row 1.	1. $25-35	2. $25-35	3. $35-45	4. $20-25	5. $15-20
Row 2.	1. $30-35	2. $30-35	3. $40-45	4. $40-45	5. $40-45 6. $10-15
	7. $15-20				
Row 3.	1. $35-45	2. $35-45	3. $35-45	4. $35-45	5. $35-45 6. $10-15
Row 4.	1. $35-40	2. $25-30	3. $25-30	4. $15-20	5. $15-20 6. $15-20
Row 5.	1. $25-30	2. $25-30	3. $25-30	4. $40-50	5. $25-30 6. $15-20
Row 6.	1. $10-12	2. $10-12	3. $10-12	4. $20-25	5. $20-25
Row 7.	1. $8-12	2. $20-25	3. $20-25	4. $25-35	5. $50-70

PLATE 10

Row 1.	1. 45-55/pr	2. 45-55/pr	3. 50-70/pr	4. $25-35	
Row 2.	1. $40-50	2. $15-20	3. $8-10		
Row 3.	1. $12-15	2. $12-15	3. $5-10	4. $5-10	
Row 4.	1. $5-10	2. $45-55	3. $25-30	4. $25-30	
Row 5.	1. $25-30	2. $8-10	3. $8-10	4. $8-10	5. $6-8
Row 6.	1. $5-10	2. $5-10	3. $5-10	4. $5-10	5. $5-10
Row 7.	1. $5-10	2. $5-10	3. $5-10	4. $12-14	5. $12-14 6. $12-14

PLATE 11

Row 1.	1. $30-35	2. $45-55	3. $15-20	4. $35-45	5. $35-45
Row 2.	1. $10-15	2. $35-45	3. $35-45	4. $35-45	5. $8-10
Row 3.	1. $8-10	2. $8-10	3. $25-35	4. $30-35	5. $30-35
Row 4.	1. $12-15	2. $20-25	3. $15-18	4. $15-18	5. $15-18
Row 5.	1. $15-18	2. $18-20	3. $20-24	4. $22-28	5. $30-35
Row 6.	1. $8-10	2. $8-10	3. $8-10	4. $8-10	5. $10-12 6. $10-12
Row 7.	1. $10-12	2. $10-12	3. $10-12	4. $18-20	5. $10-12 6. $8-10

PLATE 12

Row 1.	1. $25-35	2. $25-35	3. $35-45	4. $35-45	5. $25-30
Row 2.	1. $35-45	2. $35-45	3. $45-55	4. $25-30	5. $35-45
Row 3.	1. $35-45	2. $30-35	3. $35-45	4. $30-35	5. $30-35
Row 4.	1. $35-40	2. $15-20	3. $5-10		
Row 5.	1. $40-50	2. $45-55	3. $8-10		

PLATE 13

Row 1.	1. $20-25	2. $20-25	3. $25-30	4. $20-25	5. $20-25	
Row 2.	1. $20-25	2. $35-45	3. $20-25	4. $35-45	5. $35-45	6.$8-10
Row 3.	1. $35-45	2. $20-25	3. $20-25	4. $20-25	5. $25-30	6.$20-25
	7. $20-25					
Row 4.	1. $20-25	2. $20-25	3. $20-25	4. $20-25	5. $20-25	

PLATE 14

Row 1.	1. $25-30	2. $25-30	3. $15-20	4. $8-10	5. $8-10
Row 2.	1. $20-25	2. $20-25	3. $20-25	4. $20-25	5. $8-10
Row 3.	1. $35-45	2. $35-45	3. $50-60	4. $90-125	
Row 4.	1. $75-85	2. $20-25	3. $20-25	4. $12-15	

PLATE 15

Row 1.	1. $15-20	2. $15-20	3. $15-20	4. $15-20		
Row 2.	1. $15-20	2. $15-20	3. $15-20	4. $25-35	5. $20-25	6. $20-25
Row 3.	1. $20-25	2. $20-25	3. $15-20	4. $30-35	5. $15-20	6. $8-10
Row 4.	1. $30-35	2. $30-35	3. $30-35	4. $30-35	5. $30-35	

PLATE 16

Row 1.	1. $75-100	2. $100-150	3. $10-15	
Row 2.	1. $75-100	2. $75-100	3. $10-15	
Row 3.	1. $25-30	2. $30-45	3. $25-30	4. $20-25
Row 4.	1. $75-100	2. $75-100	3. $35-45	4. $45-55

PLATE 17

Row 1.	1. $225-250	2. $175-200	3. $175-200	4. $700-800		
Row 2.	1. $225-275	2. $250-350	3. $250-350	4. $150-195		
Row 3.	1. $300-400	2. $450-500	3. $325-375	4. $800-1000		
Row 4.	1. $200-225	2. $200-225	3. $75-100	4. $75-100	5. $150-175	6. $150-175

PLATE 18

Row 1.	1. $175-225	2. $425-475	3. $275-325	4. $20-25	
	5. $1100-1300 (Cookie House Cookie Jar Not Shown)				
Row 2.	1. $130-175	2. $80-85	3. $50-60	4. $70-75	5. $25-30
Row 3.	1. $60-70	2. $85-110	3. $55-65	4. $65-85	
Row 4.	1. $50-60	2. $90-110	3. $50-60	4. $40-50/set	5. $550-600

PLATE 19

Row 1.	1. $700-800	2. $375-425	3. $375-425	4. $375-425
Row 2.	1. $950-1100	2. $900-1000	3. $950-1000	4. $125-150
Row 3.	1. $895-1100	2.$1600-1800	3. $550-600	4. $850-950
Row 4.	1. $550-625	2. $550-625	3. $550-625	4. $550-625

PLATE 20

Row 1.	1. $525-600	2. $400-450	3. $400-450	4. $450-525
Row 2.	1. $650-700	2. $650-700	3. $600-675	4. $650-725
Row 3.	1. $700-800	2. $650-700	3. $750-800	4. $600-700
Row 4.	1. $600-650	2. $125-150	3. $950-1100	4. $450-550

PLATE 21

Row 1.	1. $95-125	2. $395-425	3. $450-495	4. $125-150
Row 2.	1. $95-125	2. $95-125	3. $295-325	4. $195-225
Row 3.	1. $400-475	2. $450-550	3. $450-550	4. $150-195
Row 4.	1. $195-225	2. $700-800	3. $550-650	4. $575-650

PLATE 22

Row 1. 1. $350-425 2. $150-175 3. $450-525 4. $95-125
Row 2. 1. $400-450 2. $450-525 3. $195-295 4. $95-125
Row 3. 1. $375-425 2. $325-395 3. $95-125   4. $1200-1400
Row 4. 1. $200-250 2. $200-250 3. $50-75   4. $150-195

PLATE 23

Row 1. 1. $30-35   2. $50-55   3. $75-80 4. $75-80   5. $30-35
Row 2. 1. $30-35   2. $15-20   3. $15-20 4. $55-65   5. $85-95   6.$100-125/se
Row 3. 1. $18-25   2. $25-30   3. $35-40 4. $55-60   5. $55-60
Row 4. 1. $55-65   2. $55-65   3. $55-65 4. $55-65   5. $55-65
Row 5. 1. $55-65   2. $55-65   3. $75-85 4. $75-85   5. $75-85
Row 6. 1. $20-25   2. $40-45   3. $40-45 4. $150-175 5. $150-200
Row 7. 1. $60-75/set 2. $50-60   3. $70-80 4. $45-50   5. $35-40

PLATE 24

Row 1. 1. $60-70   2. $30-40   3. $35-45   4. $55-65
Row 2. 1. $130-160 2. $70-80   3. $450-525 4. $175-250
Row 3. 1. $25-30   2. $35-40   3. $35-40   4. $35-40   5. $40-50 set
Row 4. 1. $100-130 2. $45-50   3. $45-50   4. $25-30   5. $35-45
Row 5. 1. $150-175 2. $150-175 3. $150-175 4. $200-225
Row 6. 1. $150-175 2. $175-250 3. $175-250 4. $200-250
Row 7. 1. $200-250 2. $50-70/set 3. $50-55 4. $40-50   5. $95-125/set

PLATE 25

Row 1. 1. $150-200 2. $175-225 3. $150-200 4. $250-275 5. $250-300
Row 2. 1. $250-275 2. $250-275 3. $150-175 4. $150-175
Row 3. 1. $250-300 2. $300-350 3. $300-325 4. $300-325
Row 4. 1. $100-150 2. $350-450 3. $350-400 4. $100-150

PLATE 26

Row 1. 1. $100-125 2. $80-100   3. $40-50   4. $250-300 5.$250-300 w/Lid
Row 2. 1. $50-60   2. $50-60   3. $40-45   4. $35-45
Row 3. 1. $40-45   2. $50-65   3. $40-45   4. $40-45
Row 4. 1. $20-25   2. $20-30   3. $50-60   4. $35-45

PLATE 27

Row 1. 1. $100-150 2. $60-75   3. $35-40   4&6. $30-35 5. $100-125
Row 2. 1. $75-100   2. $200-300 3. $100-125 4. $195-250 5. $100-150
Row 3. 1. $75-100   2. $175-225 3. $75-100 4. $75-100 5. $175-225
Row 4. 1. $300-400 2. $300-395 3. $300-350 4. $50-70
Row 5. 1. $50-75/set 2. $150-200 3. $150-200
Row 6. 1. $60-80   2. $60-80   3. $60-80   4. $60-80   5. $60-80
FIGURINES NOT SHOWN LLAMA, REINDEER, BULL DOG $80-100 each
FIGURINES WITH DECALS AND GOLD TRIM ADD $30 TO PRICE.

PLATE 28

Row 1. 1. $35-40   2. $25-30   3. $25-35   4. $80-100 5. $60-70   6. $40-50
       7. $30-35
Row 2. 1. $50-55   2. $55-60   3. $60-65   4. $75-80   5. $70-75   6. $200-225
Row 3. 1. $50-55   2. $55-65   3. $55-65   4. #90 $40-45 5. $50-55 6. $80-100/set
                                            #91 $30-35
Row 4. 1. $200-250 2. $100-110 3.$90-100   4. $55-60

Shawnee pottery items, and lines not totally illustrated

The items listed below are grouped by Shawnee's catalog numbers. They are all marked by either numbers or numbers and letters USA.

Planters #401 through #500 .... $10-20
Figural Planters #501 through #896 .... $10-20
Kenwood Lobster (Kitchen Ware) #900-935 .... $10-45
Kenwood #945 through #991 .... $15-30
Lobster (Kitchen Ware) on sundial bases $10-50
Kenwood Line #1000 through #2015 .... $10-25
Kinwood Figural Planters #2015 through #2035 .... $10-45
Liana Line #1003 through #1028 by Shawnee $10-20
Kashani Line #3000 by Kenwood Div. $10-20
Medallion Line #1500 by Kenwood Div. $10-20
Confetti Line #2100 by Kenwoood Div. $10-25
Diora Line #1600 by Shawnee $10-20
Chantilly Line #1800 by Shawnee $10-20
Petit Point Line #1900 by Shawnee... $10-30
Elegance Line #1400 by Shawnee.. $10-30
Fern Ware Line #1700 by Shawnee $10-30
Accent Line #2000 by Shawnee (Accessories) $10-45
Cameo Line #2500 by Shawnee $10-30
Cherie Line #1900 by Shawnee (Petit Point) $10-30
Touche Line #1000's by Shawnee (Liana).................................... $10-30

This Price Guide, as with most Price Guides, was designed to assist both the collector and the dealer. The prices quoted are to be used as a guide only, and were not intended to set prices. The author assumes no responsiblity for any losses that may occur as a result of consulting this book.

Typical patent reports issued for products manufactured by the Shawnee Pottery Company.

Oct. 10, 1944. R. V. GANZ Des. 139,094

COOKY JAR OR SIMILAR ARTICLE

Filed June 30, 1944 2 Sheets—Sheet 1

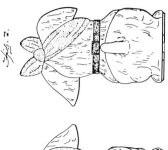

Inventor

RUDOLPH V. GANZ,

By Clarence A. O'Brien
and Harvey B. Jacobson
Attorneys

Dec. 8, 1942. R. V. GANZ Des. 134,512

COOKIE JAR

Filed Oct 9, 1942

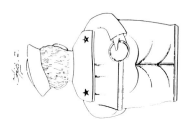

Inventor

Rudy V. Ganz

By Clarence A. O'Brien
and Harvey B. Jacobson
Attorneys

Typical patent reports issued for products manufactured by the Shawnee Pottery Company.

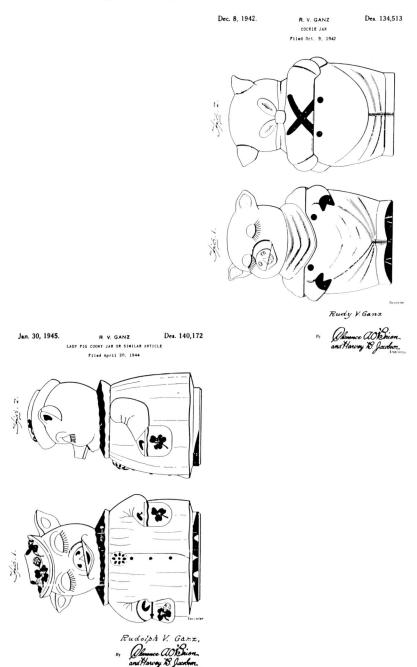

Dec. 8, 1942.   R. V. GANZ   Des. 134,513
COOKIE JAR
Filed Oct. 9, 1942

Rudy V. Ganz

Jan. 30, 1945.   R V. GANZ   Des. 140,172
LADY PIG COOKY JAR OR SIMILAR ARTICLE
Filed April 20, 1944

Rudolph V. Ganz,

Typical patent reports issued for products manufactured by the Shawnee Pottery Company.

UNITED STATES PATENT OFFICE

135,785

DESIGN FOR A SHAKER FOR SALT AND PEPPER

Rudy V. Ganz, Zanesville, Ohio, assignor to Shawnee Pottery Co., Zanesville, Ohio

Application April 27, 1943, Serial No. 110,057

Term of patent 14 years

To all whom it may concern:
Be it known that I, Rudy V. Ganz, a citizen of the United States, residing at Zanesville, in the county of Muskingum and State of Ohio, have invented a new, original, and ornamental Design for a Shaker for Salt and Pepper, of which the following is a specification, reference being had to the accompanying drawing, forming part thereof.

Figure 1 is a front elevational view of a shaker for salt and pepper, showing my new design.
Figure 2 is a side elevational view thereof.
Figure 3 is a top plan view.
I claim:
The ornamental design for a shaker for salt and pepper, as shown.

RUDY V. GANZ.

Inventor

Rudy V. Ganz

By Clarence A. O'Brien
and Harvey B. Jacobson
Attorneys

Sept. 5, 1950   J. L. PARENTICE   Des. 160,007

PLANTER

Filed Feb. 2, 1949

FIG 2

FIG 1

INVENTOR
J L PARENTICE

BY

Alyn Dee Dowell

ATTORNEY

PRESENTING THE *Riviera*

a big, big ashtray — full 17 inches across, in Mirror Black or Pure White, decorated with 22K Gold accents. Felted bottoms protect fine furniture. A conversation piece for gifts or getting — the kind of ashtray everybody wants. Individually packed in a parcel-post mailer for handling convenience.

Factory Number	Item Name	Color	Pack	Wt. per Carton	List Price
3101-B	Riviera Ashtray	Black/Gold	Individual	4 lbs	$5.00 each
3101-W	Riviera Ashtray	White/Gold	Individual	4 lbs	5.00 each

Twelve individually-packed ashtrays to a master carton, weight, 50 lbs. Please specify color when ordering. Colors may be assorted in master carton. List price is suggested retail price.

another creation by

KENWOOD **C**ERAMICS
Division of Shawnee Potteries, Zanesville, Ohio, U.S.A.

Printed in U.S.A.